LIGHT A
CREATIVE FIRE

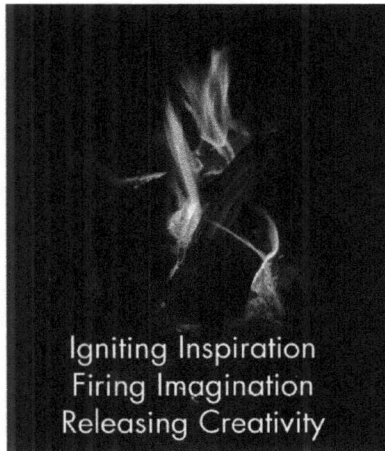

Igniting Inspiration
Firing Imagination
Releasing Creativity

J.C. Meyer

Spring Bay
Publishers

For Susie—my best friend

"This book uniquely and beautifully gives compelling insight into the relationship between human creativity and the Creator. Realizing our achievements come directly from God-given gifts, the author shows that the credits and accolades we receive should always be translated into humility and joyous praise. In so doing, we see our gifts for what they are—special blessings from our Creator to be used for His glory."

—Rosemary Matthews Franz
Portrait Artist

"J.C. Meyer's book presents a uniquely inspiring perspective on creativity. Far from being the sole purview of prodigies and the great recognized talents, Meyer conveys a compelling case that the seeds of creativity are planted in everyone, placed there by the Creator. Everything devised by human hands began as a creative idea; the same is true for the next things to come. One of those things could be in the mind of the person reading these words. To those who may think, 'I can't create anything,' perhaps it's time to rethink that. Let Meyer's book help be a catalyst."

—Geoff Koch
Composer/Film Score Producer

You were created to bring amazing and beautiful things to fruition. It's part of your DNA. We each have a unique voice, perspective, ideas and vision to transform the world around us. I love how J.C. Meyer examines human creativity in all its many forms, and then encourages and empowers all of us to simply be what God created each of us to be and become. J.C. interweaves his many thoughts and observations on creativity with a lifetime sampling of his own creations, songs, writings and vignettes. You'll enjoy his creativity and be encouraged to tap into your own creative wellspring of inspiration.

—Paul Dengler
Visual artist, Singer-songwriter,
Poet, and Forest Gump impersonator

Contents

Foreword

A re you creative? Do you write poems or songs or stories or books? Do you take photographs, sketch, draw cartoons or paint? Do you sculpt, carve, whittle, make furniture? Do you dance, tap, perform ballet? Do you sing or play a musical instrument, or both? Do you sew, knit, embroidery, weave, make jewelry?

Are you creative, or are you one of those people who look at their shoes and hopelessly mumble, "There's not a creative bone in my body." Well, don't you believe it. The book you're holding was written to change your mind about creativity and help you see that this seemingly mysterious ability is not something bestowed on a chosen few, but something we are all blessed with—and, yes, we mean blessed in the spiritual sense.

According to *LIGHT A CREATIVE FIRE*, the concept of creativity is often too narrowly defined, sort of a way of excluding people from the "creative club." The author, J.C. Meyer, believes that club would do well to have a more inclusive membership, one that recognizes and embraces all the forms of creativity that exist in this world and encourages people to become more deeply connected to their creative spirit.

It's not some Pollyannaish notion or a belief that "every kid who participates should get a trophy" that's behind the belief that creativity is a lot more widespread than we might think. The conviction comes from the author's lifetime of experience working in a creative industry, working with and around creative people, and doing more than his fair share of creating himself.

Meyer left his job as a high school music teacher in Wisconsin in the 1970s to move to Nashville. In addition to teaching others how to create and perform music, he wanted to pursue a music career of his own. He wasn't quite sure what shape that career might take, but he had faith things would work out. And they did. He spent many decades creating and producing commercial music projects for many of the country's largest and best-known brands, in addition to turning out music projects of his own.

Over the years, while he was exploring, developing and refining his own creative talents, he also was helping other people grow their creativity. There's a list of songwriters, musicians and singers—even recording engineers and soundmen—who can tell you what they learned from his direction and advice, always offered with the kind of soft-spoken humility that makes you think the suggestion was somehow your own idea.

A few years ago, Meyer started spending less time at the piano and more time at his computer, turning out insightful and inspiring posts to his blog *David's Harp*. Up to that time most of his "word writing" had been confined to song lyrics or advertising jingles that were more like songs than ads. But in *David's Harp* he found a new outlet, discovering after all these years still another place where his creative light could shine.

LIGHT A CREATIVE FIRE is a compilation of Meyer's thoughts about creativity and selections of his own artistic efforts. Drawing upon his professional career and his personal experiences, he shares his thoughts about creativity, what it is, where it comes from, how it manifests itself in our lives and our world, and how each of us, whether we realize it or not, can tap into our own creativity to lead a richer, more fulfilling life.

There's another dimension to Meyer's perspective on creativity. A person of faith, he sees a correlation between humanity's creative endeavors and those of the being who started this whole wacky universe spinning in the first place.

In a time when church attendance for all faiths is dropping and more and more people describe themselves as "spiritual but not religious," revealing one's belief in God can be risky. Still, Meyer is unabashed about his Christianity. But in *LIGHT A CREATIVE FIRE*, his spirituality is reflected in subtle "unpreaching" ways that even non-believers will find appealing.

And really, hasn't most every "creative" person—believer or not—at one time or another had a stroke of genius or brilliant inspiration that seemed to come from someplace outside themselves—something that seemed to light a creative fire that had a life of its own? If that sounds familiar, chances are the book's references to the spiritual nature of the creative process will have you nodding your head in agreement.

The basic premise of *LIGHT A CREATIVE FIRE* is that creativity is a gift generously given to each of us by the Creator himself, a gift He wants us to discover, develop and use to honor Him and enrich our lives and the lives of others. And we don't need to be a Michelangelo or a Mozart. We don't need to even do any of the typical creative things. We might be an accountant who finds beauty in numbers or a mom with a flair for baking, a lawyer preparing a legal brief or a landscaper trimming shrubs.

Whoever you are, whatever you do, this inspiring book will help you see yourself as a unique creation of a God who's given you the ability to find creativity in the world around you and in yourself, as well as the power to light a creative fire of your own that can go on burning brightly for the rest of your life.

Joe Ashley
Writer, Lyricist, Voiceover Talent
Columbus, Ohio

Jesse's Dilemma

"When everything's coming your way, you're in the wrong lane." —Anonymous

Ping! Ping! Ping! The alarm on Jesse's iPhone is going off. His arm stretches out, groping in the dark to the dresser where the phone's supposed to be. Still groggy with sleep, he pushes the phone off the dresser's top. The device clatters down the back of the dresser and lands behind it. Ping! Ping! Ping! Jesse is now on his knees on the cold floor trying to reach the phone. He utters a few choice words, finally grabs it, shuts off the alarm and staggers toward the shower.

"Where's the freakin' hot water?!" he mumbles to himself. Squeezing the last few drops from the shampoo bottle, he soaps up, rinses off, and uses yesterday's towel. Still trying to recover from his rude awakening, Jesse is suddenly aware that it's very quiet outside. The reality sinks in. "No wonder, dummy, it's Saturday," he says with a sigh.

Jesse collapses back into bed and pulls the covers over his still-wet head. But now that he's awake, it's as if the voice of a referee announces,

"False start...offense...five-yard penalty...repeat first down."

Jesse knows the bungled beginning to this Saturday morning isn't his first false start. In fact, it seems to have been his M.O. for the last several weeks. And the penalties are mounting up.

"What's wrong with me lately?" he wonders aloud. "I've been on a treadmill handling my work obligations, eating healthy, *(mostly)* and getting by, but something's just not right. I have friends and family around me, but I'm having these bouts of emptiness and unfulfillment. Something is missing, and I'm feeling out of step."

Jesse decides to tap out a text to his friend Katy to see if they can meet for coffee. Katy is always ready to listen, and her attitude is always positive. Maybe she can put her finger on what's out of sync.

"See you around mid-morning," Katy texts back. Jesse braves the cold wind as it spits snowflakes on the gray pavement and walks the three blocks to the coffee shop. Katy is already in the cashier line. She's the only customer with a smile and it's lighting up the place. She gives him a huge hug.

"Jesse, how have you been?" she asks.

"If you've got a coupla hours, I'll clue you in," he responds sardonically.

The two friends grab a booth and begin to stir the foam design out of their lattes. Jesse asks about Katy's parents and how things are going at the hospital where she works as a therapist. Their families are close, and Jesse thinks of Katy more as a sister than a friend. After a few minutes of small talk, he opens up about the empty place he finds himself in.

"I'll get to the point, Katy. I'm going through the motions," says Jesse. "Nothing seems to give me a feeling that I matter or that I'm heading in the right direction. I teach my classes and I enjoy the kids, but if I would grade my performance, I'd give myself a D, maybe an Incomplete."

"Don't be so hard on yourself, Jesse," Katy remarks, looking concerned. "You got high marks on your classroom review, and the faculty gave you added responsibilities."

"I wish that would encourage me, Katy, but something's just missing. It feels like I'm on auto-pilot, mindlessly going from task to task."

Katy looks perplexed. "I realize you gave up law school when..."

"Going into law was my dad's idea, Katy, not mine," Jesse interrupts. "He doesn't bring up law school much these days. But he often remarks about how much time I spend making up songs and playing in a band every weekend. He says it'll end up going nowhere, and he's probably right."

"So you changed your major to get an education degree," Katy points out. "You've got that going for you. I came out to hear the band several times and thought the songs you wrote were really good."

Jesse leans in and half-whispers, "Welcome to my dilemma, Katy. Getting into the music business is like walking through a mine field. I really do like to write, but..."

"Then you have to make a choice of what you want to pursue," Katy says. "Teaching is something you're obviously good at, and it'll pay the bills. But what are you most passionate about?"

Immediately Jesse becomes animated. Glancing around the coffee shop as if to make sure no one is eavesdropping, he lowers his voice: "I'll let you in on a little secret, Katy. A friend of mine's dad is opening up a car dealership, and asked me to write a radio commercial, you know, a jingle. If he likes it, he'll put it on the air!"

"Well that explains it," Katy says with a smile. "Sounds like opportunity is knocking."

"I should be spending this weekend grading papers, but writing this commercial is all I can think about."

"Sounds like you're asking me for advice," says Katy. "I'm like Lucy in the Peanuts comic strip. My sign is up—Psychiatrist 5¢."

Jesses laughs. "At five bucks for your latte, your fee is still a bargain."

"So here's my take," Katy continues. "I know you pretty well, at least well enough to be able to tell you not to take yourself so *seriously.* Everyone has to make choices about changes; so choose to follow the path you're passionate about."

"I started out as an RN and ended up a therapist because it felt like it would be more rewarding. I also prayed about the move before taking that next step and it has worked out beautifully. Have you considered asking for answers upstairs?"

"I could have, but that seemed more like a last resort," Jesse admits. "Besides, I wasn't sure I should be having these feelings."

"It sounds to me like you're dealing with some false guilt," Katy replies. "God has a way of getting us where he wants us. He puts people in our path who redirect us to where he intended. Maybe your car dealer friend's offer is part of his plan."

"And so are you, Katy. I gave you a call, and you answered and you were willing to meet and encourage me. Thanks for being a true friend! Maybe I can return the favor someday."

"I've got to run home before my shift starts at noon," Katy tells him, giving his hand a squeeze. "You'll be fine, whatever you decide. Ask for guidance."

They part ways with a promise to stay in touch.

Jesse spent the rest of that weekend grading papers, setting aside time to come up with an idea for the radio commercial. The following Monday he presented a clever song he wrote for the dealership and saw the manager's eyes light up when he heard it. *All systems go.*

Jesse lined up a session date with the guys in his band, and gave them the news that this would be a paying gig. *(woohoo!)* They had a quick rehearsal to work out their parts.

When the day arrived, Jesse walked into the studio for his first-ever recording session. The room seemed to hold a kinetic energy within its walls, a certain vibe.

Once they'd gotten used to a headphone mix and the wires and mic lines snaking everywhere, it took the guys three or four rundowns to settle into a groove that timed out at sixty seconds. Then the Record light went on, the drummer counted off—*a one, two, three, four*—and the music began to flow. Listening back, Jesse and his bandmates agreed that it was a great take. After the vocal overdubs and a final mix, they called it a wrap. *High fives all around.*

One day not long after that, as Jesse was driving to school, the car dealer spot began playing on his radio. He was totally floored when he heard it. In fact, he realized after it was over that he had also floored the gas pedal and was now twenty miles over the speed limit. Jesse somehow felt like a secret door had opened up inside of him.

"You must be telling me something, God, about where you want me," he thought aloud.

Several weeks later, it was Katy who needed support from Jesse. An eight-year-old boy who was her patient in therapy had taken a turn for the worse and died. She was distraught and reached out to Jesse to help her through her grief. He was led to remind her that all of life is in God's hands, a thought that stuck with him. Inspired by what had happened, the next day Jesse wrote a song for Katy:

Jesse's Dilemma

Got your message on my phone
It sounded like a cry for help
When I heard your S O S
I was a little distressed myself
You've always been the stronger one
Ready to handle whatever comes
You were telling me just the other day

Chorus:
Be ready for what God can do
Be ready—his hands are shaping you
Not a single wasted motion
You're his labor of love

Be ready—he'll make the pieces fit
'Cause he's not finished with you yet
Nothing can undo
What God can do

Took a cross-town taxi
Rang the bell at the top of the stair
Hoping I could ease your pain
Just by being there
Isn't life full of surprises
When the blind lead the ones that see
I was putting into practice
What you were preaching to me

(Repeat Chorus)

Nothing can undo...
What God can do

After putting the finishing touches on it, Jesse sent Katy the song. It was the first time he had written a song for someone else's benefit. He was beginning to feel the weight and power of words, and it was rocking his world.

****

This story of Jesse and Katy is a work of fiction, based on real life experiences. Conventional wisdom always tells you to write about what you know. I've taken dramatic license to raise awareness of the bigger picture of what it means to be creative.

The more I've been involved with people in various walks of life and sharing their experiences, the more immense creativity has become. The more I am made aware of the way God bestows multi-faceted talents and skills, and the more glorious I see them shine. I hope that will be true for you, too.

May what follows inspire you to consider opening up your world to deeper experiences of God's beauty and purpose when you LIGHT A CREATIVE FIRE, one that makes you...uniquely you.

Fred's shed

Igniting Inspiration

Nothing is more intimidating to a writer than a blank page. Like a woodworker making their first cut on a chunk of wood, or a painter's first stroke on a blank canvas, a person who puts thoughts on paper must begin to scrawl.

Both Jesse and Katy, in the previous story, wrestled with what role they would play, one that would feel like the right response to where they felt led.

So it is with you. Anything creative will only come to life when you find the passion to pursue it. You may dismiss the urge until you come up against an idea or thought that won't leave you alone until you address it. This prompting is *inspiration,* and as you will see, it can be more than an urge; it can be a requirement calling on you to bring it to life.

More than you realize, inspiration has few boundaries. Teaching a class, writing a speech or a diary entry, making a sketch, or a business plan are all triggered by *inspiration*. Consider your engagement in skillful endeavors—cooking,

13

gardening, interior decorating, singing, playing an instrument, crafts and hobbies—and you're soon surrounded by a host of creative gifts.

What Was Revealed in Creation

Since the beginning of time, nothing has surpassed the work of the Master Creator. He gave his Spirit, his inspiration (*from the Latin inspirare, meaning to breathe into*) to Adam and Eve, and they became living beings. God delighted in what he created so much, he called them *"very good."*

That makes us humans the crown of his creation. Realize also that we are on speaking terms with him, along with the rest of his creation, to lift up our prayers and praises to him. That's why he fashioned us—for him to love us well and for us to celebrate him.

Do you realize there's a hum in the universe? It comes from the sound of the cosmos giving glory to its Creator in many different frequencies, many decibels far above and below what our ears can hear. King David, in his role as psalmist, was inspired to write in Psalm 148:

"Praise him, sun and moon! Praise him, all you twinkling stars! Praise him, skies above! Let every created thing give praise to the Lord, for he issued his command, and they came into being."

Then the Scripture, Genesis 1, tells us: *"In the beginning God created the heavens and the earth. And God said..."*

City ballet

Light a Creative Fire

I want light to come out of darkness
I want skies to touch the sea
A place for the land and a place for the heavens
So God said let there be
And there was
God said let there be
And there was

I want grass carpets and vegetation
I want flowers and plants and trees
In every color and shape I can imagine
So God said let there be
And there was
God said let there be
And there was

I want sun and stars and a moon to encircle
To illumine the day and rule the night
I want birds to fly and fish to swim
To fill sky and sea and multiply

I want creatures shaggy and smooth
To climb and run and cover the land
And this was how the world began
God said let there be
And there was
God said let there be
And there was

Energized by God's Word

I f you want to know the heart and mind of God, you'll find them in Scripture, the inspired word of God. Some who are not yet believers will dispute the *inspired* part, saying that the Bible is a good road map for moral living, or a collection of stories drawn from the history of God's people. Nothing more.

These are the same people who say Jesus was a great teacher and a good moral compass, but miss the point. The Bible came into being when holy men were given the *breath* of God, and were *inspired to write it*. Beginning with Genesis 3:15, the first promise, the life of Jesus, the coming Messiah, is the God-breathed thread that runs through the entire Bible to the final chapter of Revelation.

Think of the red or gold bookmark string in your Bible. Wherever you place it between the pages, you'll read how God the Father stretches out his guiding hand as he oversees the Old Testament patriarchs, the Children of Israel, the coming of his Son Jesus, his life, death, and resurrection, then how the work of the early church was led by the Holy Spirit who energized the disciples with a holy fire at Pentecost. Talk about the breath of God!

When you sit and read any good book, it's like entering into a movie in your mind. What you envision captures a story, a mood, a time and a place. God the Creator places these imaginings in your mind's eye, making them come alive as you read his Word. What images come to you as you read the following verses:

The Song Inside

A broken melody – plays inside my head
Jumbled thoughts unravel line by line
Is it voices of angels – or pieces of dreams
Words escape me – nothing comes to mind

Rhythms tumble – they spin
They curve the air – they pull me in
Dropping down from heaven knows where

Create in me – the song inside
Let it see the light of day – bring it to life
Lord shape it with your hand
Breathe your spirit in
Give the song inside me wings to fly

Help me paint with words – until the colors run
Without you only empty black and white
Come on in – make yourself at home
Empty pages wait for me to write

I'm letting go what I've been holding in
The rocks the trees the hills are joining in
It's like the whole world wants to sing

Create in me – the song inside
Let it see the light of day – bring it to life
Lord shape it with your hands
Breathe your spirit in
Give the song inside me wings to fly

© 2014 Selah Music (From David's Harp/The Song
Inside You)

The Role of the Holy Spirit

Just to be clear, God *is* the Holy Spirit. Together with Jesus and the Father, the Holy Spirit inspires us. Like a wind that blows the tree branches, we only see the result of the wind as it moves through the trees. So it is when the Holy Spirit breathes.

Every time you've felt the words you were reading from Scripture come alive, you were experiencing the Holy Spirit's *"inspiring"*, breathing in. The same thing happens when you find an answer to a problem after praying about it. God welcomes your prayer, and sends the Holy Spirit to carry out a solution, often revealing it in mysterious ways. Here are just a few of his responses:

- Young Samuel heard a voice three times during the night and ran to tell Eli the priest. Finally Eli told him to say, "Speak Lord, your servant is listening."
- Noah conversed with God who gave him exact dimensions for the ark.
- Joseph dreamt his brother's sheaves bowed down to his sheaves.
- Gideon determined God's answer by finding dew on wool fleece.

- Daniel interpreted signs and dreams for King Nebuchadnezzar.
- Abraham heard God speak to him from a burning bush.
- John wrote the whole book of Revelation from visions.
- Joseph was told three different times in dreams: to accept Mary as his wife, to flee to Egypt, and to return to Nazareth.
- God gave Balaam's donkey the ability to speak out for being beaten unfairly.
- Every book of the Bible was transcribed by inspired holy men.

Often it's an interruption of the status quo by the Holy Spirit that energizes the creative process. You may have been ignoring a need to express yourself, or neglecting to search for a creative outlet, or just waiting for inspiration. This feeling of a presence by the Holy Spirit prompting you to take action is yours for the asking. That's how this lyric ended up being written, a time when it felt like God walked through the room.

Igniting Inspiration

Let Your Spirit Flow
Like an oasis in the desert
Like a harbor in a raging sea
Like a father's open arms
Your love surrounded me

I'm carried along by the current
In the spirit of love we are one
From my heart – from my soul
Let your spirit flow

Chorus:
May you always be my one desire
Fill me with your inner fire
Let your spirit flow
When I need strength to carry on
When there's joy – joy in my song
Living water for my thirsting soul
Let your spirit flow

Fill me O Lord from your fountain
Pour me out on those in need
For those who still don't know
Let your spirit flow

When I fall, when I falter, forgive me
When my supply is running low
Refresh me with your inspiration
Let your spirit flow

© 1987 Selah Music

Light a Creative Fire

Through the hum of creation, through the Word, through the mysterious workings of the Holy Spirit, we are summoned to *do life* in the presence of our Creator. He seeks to inspire you and stir your imagination, to bless you with the ability to be creative and resourceful, and to bestow on you a completeness you will find only in Him.

As you remove your barriers to creative freedom, you'll begin to roam free in the imaginings of God. You will soon find you are being called on to be his witness.

Pickin' parlor

Firing Imagination

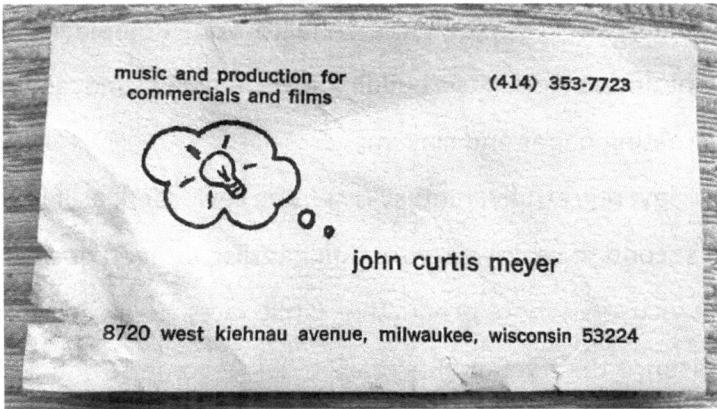

music and production for
commercials and films

(414) 353-7723

john curtis meyer

8720 west kiehnau avenue, milwaukee, wisconsin 53224

When inspiration beckons, it's like lightning in a bottle; it sparks your *imagination.*

It is this stimulation of your mind that generates creativity and resourcefulness. Thoughts are sifted and sorted until you find solutions that feel like answers. Through trial and error or experience, you learn from your failures to capture success. All are included in the process of arriving at creativity's Aha moment. *Viola! That's it!*

Fantasy Versus Reality

Your mind has the natural ability to be creative and resourceful. When you were growing up, you played store, dressed up in mom or dad's clothes, and drew pictures inspired by stories that were read to you. Roleplaying is imagination at work. So is building forts, making sandcastles, and creating paper and clay images.

Today, regretfully, fantasy is seldom rewarded, as if it's a poor second to reality. Daydreaming is discouraged because being focused is more productive, while facts are given more importance than fiction. Recreation has become structured, while free play is frowned on because it doesn't produce measurable results.

As a result, the vivid imaginings we used to dream up are lost. Most of what we see is already illustrated for us. Movies, video games, and TV, by filming or animating just about everything, have made us watchers instead of imaginers. In today's world, you can sit and watch what the whole world is doing, compliments of Google, Xbox, and the Internet.

Unfortunately, more illustration only makes life more complex. But as technology becomes more invasive, this emerging worldview can serve your imagination and deepen your experiences. It's up to you to choose what you want to see and hear. Like a screen with twelve thousand channels, you're often bombarded with more real life than you want, some of which isn't good for you.

Scientists predict the future will be run by artificial intelligence. But I know of a God *who is* and *will always be* in control of the world we live in. There will always be a need for a sound mind and a fertile imagination. God will see to it.

When I start taking a changing world too seriously, mixing in a little levity always seems to help. By writing in fantasy, I'm telling myself... *lighten up!*

More than I Want to Know

As I was leaving for work I gave her a kiss (I said)
Honey did you pay the bills and she said this
The credit cards maxed out and the rent's overdue
I need money for groceries and tuition for school
And I said oops, sorry honey, I've gotta go
You're telling me more than I want to know

I went out for lunch and ran into a friend
I said hey good buddy how have you been
And he went off about his son's baseball team
This kid can hit and he fields like a dream
And I said oh—look at the time, I've gotta go
He was telling me more than I want to know

Picked up the paper on the way home
The news wasn't good—guess I should have known
Global warming—economy's slowing
My teams are losing—deficits growing
Couldn't get past the front page before it got old
Always telling me more than I want to know

Bridge:
I've got magazines—more than I'll ever read
Eight hundred stations on my cable TV
Radio talk shows twenty-four seven
I'm drowning in a sea of information
Yada yada yada—blah blah blah

I'll listen to someone who'll think twice
Before they say what's on their mind
Who'll have a point when they talk – that would be nice
Silence is golden – at least some of the time
Then words will have meaning—I'll say is that so
Tell me more – I want to know
© 2006 Selah Music

On a clear day

Generating Imagination

It's 5:10 am. Outside everything is in various shades of gray. The house is quiet. The only sound is the ticking of a pendulum clock and the scratching of my pen. I scribble down the side of a blank piece of paper so at least the ink starts flowing. Every creative venture begins with unharnessing your thoughts so they can run free.

I'm sifting through some words that came from a conversation the night before. I write them down. They stick with me because words have a certain weight, and I want to measure them. It really is okay to be curious, to follow where your thoughts take you.

Pearls of wisdom often come from an irritating grain of sand. One of the words that resonates with me is *empathy*, the ability to understand and share the feelings of others. Empathy requires you to get outside of yourself and use it as a building block of imagination.

Knowledge builds empathy for other cultures and ways of life by gathering experiences through traveling, or reading, or simply by being observant. Imagine another's point of view until it falls on paper through you, the one pushing the pen.

Four people go to a play. When asked what they liked best, a designer will praise the set design, a seamstress will rave about the costumes, a musician will go on about the score, while an actor will offer a critical appraisal of the characters' stage presence and diction. Not everyone sees things the same way, and that is as God intended.

Let a Godly focus be a filter for your imagination. I call it putting on your God glasses, so you can see things in his perspective and dismiss any negative thoughts that come from the Evil One. Shine up your reflection of Jesus; ask him to be a co-creator that will influence what you create. He will honor that prayer every time you ask.

Take every chance to entertain ideas that spur your imagination. Keep a sketchbook handy. Doodling is allowed. Write down hot button words that for some reason stay with you. Keep a journal. Take pictures. Take lessons or classes. Listen to others and ask questions. Read, read, read. Actress Lauren Bacall once said, *"Imagination is the highest kite that one can fly."*

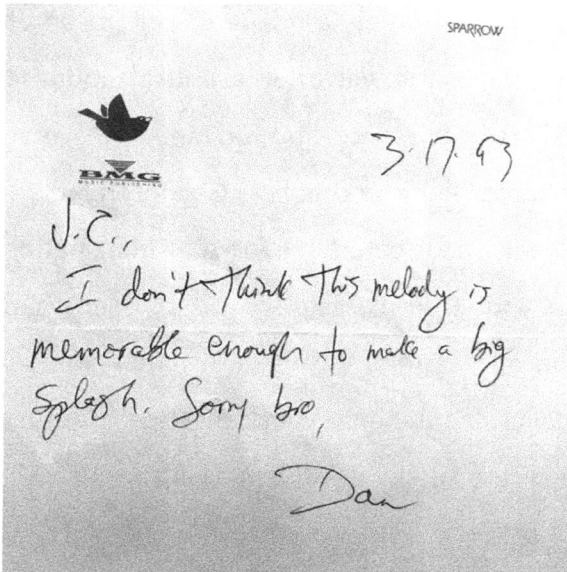

SPARROW

3.17.93

J.C.,

I don't think this melody is memorable enough to make a big splash. Sorry bro,

Dan

Be prepared, for whatever you create may not be well received. Use a response like the one above to motivate you to go back to the drawing board. Every idea must go through a refining process, and if your idea hits a brick wall, take off in another direction. You might feel led to create something that's radically ahead of its time.

Trust your instincts. Stick to your guns. If your initial idea seems startling, you may choose to rein it in. Stay loose. Consider all avenues. Shape and reshape, until you feel that sensation that speaks to you, that stays with you. Let it sit for a few days; when you revisit it, you'll know whether it's worthy, whether it's a piece of yourself.

Making Imagination Your Platform

You've heard talk about being left-brained, that is, having a convergent mind, or being right-brained, also called divergent intelligence. Left-brained persons are more analytical and focus on sequential thoughts. Right-brained individuals are freethinkers and are more creative and less concerned about boundaries.

People who measure such tendencies and human traits will be the first to tell us that left-brained and right-brained behavior is frequently both/and. (*BTW, you're free to analyze this, even if you're more right-brained.*) If you're asking why people are this way, the short answer is that God loves variety.

You've been given a totally unique, one-of-a-kind identity. No one else is like you or has the same combination of gifts or the same feelings. In certain ways, thinking outside of the proverbial box is the beginning of imaginative solutions that lead to change. George Bernard Shaw was the one who said, *"Some see things as they are and say why. I dream things that never were and say why not?"*

God can and will use certain people to push past boundaries and accomplish what goes against accepted norms. Imagine what chaos and scorn came from the lives of Noah, or Samson, or Jehu the fanatical king, or John the Baptist. God allowed them to receive thoughts that accomplished his purposes.

He builds character and personality into each of our lives that *demonstrate* who he is. So don't hold on too tightly to your self-image, because the talents and gifts he gives you are for *his* glory. The happiest people I know are those who have found they've been given a servant's heart, one that is open to sharing themselves with others.

"Do you have the gift of speaking? Then speak as though God himself were speaking through you. Do you have the gift of helping others? Do it with all the strength and energy that God supplies. Then everything you do will bring glory to God through Jesus Christ" (1 Peter 4:11).

The New Me
*Left my human nature in the closet
Today I'll wear you like a garment
With you so close it gives me joy*

*I feel the strength of you around me
A certain sweetness
The blessed completeness
Of a perfect fit
Oh this—this is the new me*

*Carved in your image
Captured in your imagination
Shining for the rest of the world
This is the new me*

© 2019 Selah Music

"Man's chief end is to glorify God and to enjoy him forever."
—Westminster Shorter Catechism

Prayer chapel

Releasing Creativity

Tokens of Your Love

When discussing inspiration, I referred to being a witness. It's an awareness that you're living out your life's story for all to see. It's about being willing to share the talents and skills you've been given for the benefit of others with the kind of creativity that has your unique stamp on it.

My mother was a china painter. She didn't pursue her artistic side until she was in her early fifties; she was too busy raising kids and holding our family together. She blossomed into an artist, creating many sought-after pieces she displayed at art fairs and craft gatherings. She taught china painting to students in weekly classes until her last days.

Her pieces are displayed all around our house and in the homes of many others, and I remember her every time I see them and admire her work. Each one is a legacy to the God-given gift she shared. Each one is a token of her love.

When you create using your unique talents, there's something sacred about it. While some will take credit for what is fashioned from their inspiration and imagination, their mind, their thoughts, their artistic eye, all are just clay shaped by hands of the Potter.

He will accomplish whatever he chooses with your gifts. He expects us to manifest himself through our works and our lives and actions. It's a humbling experience to be in sync with him, to be used by God, as his hands, his feet, his artistic expression. Being his witness is simply a token of your love for him.

Almost two decades ago, I took notes on a book by Leland Ryken called *The Liberated Imagination*[1] that resonated with me. He wrote a treatise on what a Theistic worldview was, that *"God is the reference point of all experiences – the one who gives meaning and identity to all of life."* God blessed Leland with that gift of expressive writing so he could share God's glory. It inspired me to write this song lyric years later as a response...

Center of the Universe

You are every star that shines
The center of the universe
You speak and planets fall in line
With the center of the universe
You arranged them all so perfectly
In flawless synchronicity
Like diamonds they illuminate your majesty
You're the center of the universe

You're a glorious symphony
Playing throughout the universe
Ten thousand angels accompany
To the applause of the universe
The God of all lifts up my soul
The Spirit falls it overflows
I see Jesus when my eyes are closed
At the center of the universe

All of life revolves around you
Lord be the all in all I do
Lead me on my earthly journey to
The center of the universe

© 2019 Selah Music

The Joy of Creating

Creativity is like currency—you're spending yourself for others, and in turn you receive the joy of sharing as a bonus.

God needs to get things done, so he provides a way for those who have certain skills or talents to blossom. The Bible calls it *raising up*—anointing skillful leaders, brave warriors, women with a selfless heart for God. Recall how he recruited everyday people—fishermen, tax collectors, even a physician—endowing them with credentials to be his disciples and, later on, builders of the early church.

You are no different. You have special talents and skills that he has placed in your DNA, that shape your personality. I can imagine the Creator going down a list and saying, "She's going to be my teacher; that one's got great maternal instincts; he's going to be a great influence on people; this one will be a naturalist..."

The Creator of the universe has no boundaries or limits to what he's capable of creating. He loves diversity, almost to the point of being outrageous. This is the same God who created a billion galaxies of a billion stars each, then turned his attention to snowflakes, making each one different than the other.

Releasing Creativity

Many times what we imagine is problem-solving, a way to create order out of chaos. That's how scrap lumber cut to just the right lengths becomes a storage shed. That's how leftover material and old T-shirts are turned into a quilt that'll brighten up a bedroom. Clearing a patch of weedy ground is the first step to creating a garden that will grow a harvest of fresh produce.

Do you create artistic bear and deer images using a chainsaw? *More power to ya.* Do you love to cook and bake and bang around pots and pans in the kitchen? *Save a taste for me.* Do you love ballroom dancing, or the polka? *Then shake a tail feather!*

All these and more are the expression of inspiration, imagination, and creativity. God has bestowed on us a panorama of style and diversity. No holds barred!

He gathers his creation to serve his purposes, and to carry out creative works of service and caring that meet the needs of families, neighbors, even strangers all around us. What are the ways you can use your creativity to be a blessing to those around you?

Here's a short list: befriend, visit, teach, pray for, bake for, entertain, sing to, sew for, exercise with, encourage, repair stuff, do excellent work for, tell stories to, listen to, laugh with, cry with, care for, and on and on.

I Was Made for This

A painter works on canvas
A poet speaks in rhyme
A potter's wheel shapes the clay
Into his unique design

Make me strong so I can hold you
Take and shape me as you will
I'll be your willing vessel
Waiting to be filled

I'll pour out your beauty
A witness to your bliss
Oh I—I was made for this

© 2019 Selah Music

5...4...3...2...1...

Coming to Fruition

Following creative pursuits begins by sorting out the activities that interest you, ones that seem to come naturally. Those activities you keep coming back to because you enjoy them are *"your thing."* Whatever challenges your mind, whatever feels right in your hands, release them as a celebration of the One who provides them.

Try not to measure your skills and talents by the world's standards. We've got enough vanity and self-aggrandizement in the world as it is. If it's artsy, or crafty, or just beautiful in your eyes, if creating it makes you happy, just do it. People will welcome the gifts you share even more when you offer them modestly, with humility, and with a willing spirit.

That wise philosopher Will Rogers said, *"We can't all be heroes, because somebody has to sit on the curb and clap as they go by."* We all want to make a difference with what we've created. But after accolades and applause fades, it's the joy and satisfaction you find when you put your heart into it that satisfies.

Creativity is a form of worship. I grew up with a hymn that says, *"Take my hands and let them move — At the impulse of Thy love."* When a thought or idea or inspiration comes unexpectedly, pursue it as if it were divine intervention. It's an honor to be a tool in God's hands, being used for his glory and knowing that you're expressing the joy and beauty and the awesomeness of God as his image-bearer.

Your best work often comes from your most challenging undertakings. Irish novelist Samuel Beckett said, *"Try again, fail again, fail better."* You may be stretched by a learning curve as you finetune your talents, but hang in there. You'll learn from every redo, remake, and revision as you fashion a thing of beauty, of purpose, of function.

The glory of God resides within you. You're a living, walking, working expression of the one who owns your heart.

Philippians 1:6: *"And I am certain that God, who began the good work within you, will continue his work until it is finally finished on the day when Christ Jesus returns"* (St. Paul the Apostle).

Ever since God created the universe, he's never stopped creating. I hope you've come to realize, so it is with you. You're his work in progress, and every plan or thought or idea or solution is his imagination and creativity coming to fruition *through you*. He is the cornerstone of creativity and inspiration and art, every brush stroke, every design, every craft and idea. He is sending out his light through you.

****

What follows is a Baskin Robbins® 31 flavors approach to story songs I've written, some I've labeled street ballads or lyric poems, some romantic, some whimsical, some poignant. Only a few have ever been pitched to publishers. I wasn't much for writing about breaking hearts, or cheating songs, or about loving my truck, making me an unknown quantity for Nashville's country music handlers.

Without judging others or being prudish, I've always felt creating dark themes for a troubled world was redundant. I'd rather share positive life experiences and observations. But that's just me. For some, that's too narrow a focus; they want to push beyond boundaries. Find *your true self* and draw from what you know, your experiences, what makes you curious, or what you're passionate about.

Wherever your creative focus takes you, God not only brings the inspiration you need, but also provides a springboard to your imagination. And yes, it is most appropriate to pray and ask for directions. He *will* get you where he wants you.

Releasing Creativity

Because you are God's workmanship, anything you create, design, build, or prepare is kindled by a spark that comes from within. It's an energy he's given you – your gifts, your talents, your natural ability, that promises to burst into flame when you *LIGHT A CREATIVE FIRE*.

Story Songs

"God created man because he loves stories." —Elie Wiesel, author of Night

Across the Border
Every day he comes down to the wall
Hoping she will be there
In the bitter cold before nightfall
From a distance he can see her
She waves to him from the other side
And with his eyes he holds her
With a love so strong it builds a bridge
Across the border

Divided homeland torn in two
Barricades and barbed wire
No risk of danger can undo
Two lives in the line of fire
Boundaries forcing them apart
Passion pulls between two hearts
When love's this strong it builds a bridge
Across the border

Remember how we'd dream of life
In a land of milk and honey
Until one day our dream came true
When the walls came tumbling down

Now we're fighting our own private war

Light a Creative Fire

Like there's a wall between us
And as the battle lines are drawn
Our feelings leave us speechless
Can we agree to call a truce
Can we talk things over
And find the love that built a bridge
Love strong enough to build a bridge
Across the border

© 2009 Selah Music

****

Recycled Ts (Barb Schoenbeck)

Light a Creative Fire

"Everything you can imagine is real."
—Pablo Picasso

First Love
I saw an old man—along the side of the road
Said his truck broke down—it was rainy and cold
Throw your bags in the back—put my extra coat on
We'll see if we can find some help when we get to town

I saw his long gray beard—and I noticed his hands
They didn't look rough and calloused—like a truck-driving man's
Said he was making deliveries—must have been UPS
Trying to find the ones who left—no forwarding address

That would be me I said—I've been traveling around
It's been over two years since I left my father's farm
I thought the grass was greener and man was I ever wrong
To this day I wish I had never left home

Cause that was my first love—the life we had
That farm and my family—especially my dad
We had land—we had cattle—we worked sun-up 'til sun-down
I thought that kind of life—happened to everyone

So I took it all for granted—my first love became myself
I demanded my inheritance—my portion of my father's wealth
I got lost in the nightlife—wine, women and song
One day I woke up—and everything was gone

So like I said I've been traveling around
I work wherever I can—and take life the way it comes
Every good thing I ever had—slipped right through my hands
My first love's just a memory—and what could have been

Story Songs

Then the old man spoke—you can still settle the score
From what you've told me—I don't have to hear any more
I was sent by your father to see if you've changed
You passed your first test when you picked me up in the rain

Drop me off here—you'll want to go south
You've taken the long way—now take the shortest route
Your father's been waiting—to welcome you home
A father's first love—is for his wayward son

****

****

"And while he was still a long way off, his father saw him coming. Filled with love and compassion, he ran to his son, embraced him and kissed him" (Luke 15:20).

****

Light a Creative Fire

"Life isn't about waiting for the storm to pass. It's about learning how to dance in the rain."
—Unknown

The best thing about a new day is that it gives us a chance to start over.

Lighten up Amigo
Woke up this morning
My dog was smiling
Standing on my chest licking my face
He didn't care about the mess
I made of yesterday
If he had his master's voice
He'd look at me and say

Chorus:
Lighten up amigo
Give me a smile
And brighten up my day
Lighten up amigo
It's gonna come together
Today will be better
It's gonna work out
Just go with the flow
Oh ohhhh lighten up

I got my feet to touch the floor
Heard her voice outside my door
Asking me if everything was okay
She had every right to be
Expecting an apology
She had every reason
To put me in my place
But she said

Story Songs

Lighten up amigo
Give me a smile
And brighten up my day
Lighten up amigo
It's gonna come together
Today will be better
It's gonna work out
Just go with the flow
Oh ohhhh lighten up

So when you're having one of those days
When everything ends up sideways
Against the current and the crashing waves
When the fun goes out of what life could be
I've got a sure-fire remedy

Lighten up amigo
Give me a smile
And brighten up my day
Lighten up amigo
It's gonna come together
Today will be better
It's gonna work out
Just go with the flow
Oh ohhhh lighten up

* * * * * * * * * * * * * * * * * *

Light a Creative Fire

I grew up in a blue-collar town. One of the people on my paper route, old Mr. Johnson, lived alone in a creepy old house that I used as the model for this story. I never went inside because I always gave him his paper at his customary seat at the Lakeside Tavern, but I could imagine it.

This Old House
I saw this old house—passing by one day
The porch was sagging—weeds were overgrown
Seems whoever lived here—just walked away
The door was open—no one was home

I asked a neighbor—said it was for sale
Thought it wouldn't hurt—to have a look around
Walls needed painting—carpets were worn
The roof was leaking—letting in the rain

Chorus:
It wasn't much to look at—this old house
But something was drawing me to this old house
I'll bring her by and show her
How we could turn this place around
There's a lot of living left in this old house

She cried the first time—she saw this old house
She made me wonder—was it really that bad
Through her tears she told me—it looks so lonely
Still it's more than—we ever had

Chorus:
She said it's not much to look at—this old house
But something's drawing me to this old house
It'd be a roof over our heads
And a leaky one at that
So when are we moving in to this old house

Story Songs

We swept out the sadness – the old broken dreams
Repaired the roof—re-stained the kitchen floor
What we uncovered—was a heart and soul
The kind you'll feel when—you walk in the door

Chorus:
It took on a life of its own—this old house
There's something you can't buy in this old house
If you asked me what we found there
It was about the love we shared
And the stories that we made
In this old house

© 2010, 2019 Selah Music

"I've learned that people will forget what you said, people will forget what you did, but people will never forget how you made them feel."—Maya Angelou

****

Light a Creative Fire

I wrote and produced a piece for a photography association called "Remember with Pictures." This song came from that experience; running like a video in my head. Some experiences are from years ago, yet they may feel as if they happened just yesterday.

Pictures
Some are in color / some are black and white
Some are out of focus / some have streaks of light
Some reveal the truth / while others tell a lie
Here's me sayin'...bye

Some are from last summer / some from long before
Some have much too ceiling / some have too much floor
Some are tear-stained / some make you wonder why
Here's me sayin'...bye

Bridge:
Some go in the album / some go in the drawer
Some go on the mirror / some hang by the door
Some the only proof of the way it used to be
The way it used to be

Some make you smile / some make you sad
Some are just too precious / some you wish you never had
'Cause some are just too painful to look at any more
Here's one of you as you're walking out the door
Here's me sayin'...bye

© 1997 Selah Music

****

Watergate

Light a Creative Fire

Elmer Gantry was a feature film about a con man and a female evangelist selling religion to small-town America, based on a novel by Sinclair Lewis. I recall wondering whether it was fact or fiction...

Revival's Comin'

Send out the fliers and pass the word
Revival's comin' to town
Put up the tent and put the sawdust down
Revival's comin' to town

Put up the whisky—no more shakin' dice
All the ladies gonna dress extra nice
At least 'til the tent comes down
Revival's comin' to town

Been no rain forty days and nights
But revival's comin' to town
Been no work at the mill—lots of time to kill
But revival's comin' to town

Maybe it's time to be sayin' some prayers
Sing some old hymns and shed some tears
Get right with God 'cause the end is near
Revival's comin' to town

Those nights the choir began to sing
Those who came started feeling everything
From pain to joy—from despair to hope
From the fires of hell to heaven's gain

And when the tents were folded
God must've looked down
Cause the mills been starting to hire again
And the rain's been steadily comin' down
What was lost somehow's been found
Ever since revival came to town

© 2009 Selah Music

Story Songs

"Showing no concern for the uncertainties that lie ahead is the secret of walking with Jesus."—Oswald Chambers

What would it be like if your life was hanging in the balance, knowing your life would be taken for what you believe?

Deepest Devotion
Under cover of the night
Outside the city gates
We take the winding path to the catacombs
We're sure to be arrested
If we're ever followed here
Since Peter's disappearance
We've been living in fear

Chorus:
But tonight—tonight
We'll gather in the candlelight
To hear the words the Master has spoken
Tonight—tonight
All we can give is our deepest devotion
Deepest devotion

It's the morning after
In the city square
We hear approaching hoof beats
Roman soldiers everywhere
We offer no resistance
As we're bound and chained like thieves
We're led to the prison chambers
And find Peter on his knees

Chorus:
And tonight—tonight
We'll pray with Peter in the fading light
That our spirits will not be broken
Tonight—tonight

Light a Creative Fire

All we can give is our deepest devotion
Deepest devotion

It's the morning of the third day
We're led to the arena
We see the rows of crosses
But we have no fear
And as the flames surround us
We feel God's arms around us
He gathers us unto himself
And the world disappears

Chorus:
And tonight—tonight
Though centuries have passed
We sing the martyr's song
With deep emotion
And that day will come
We'll all stand at his throne
And give our deepest devotion
Endless devotion (repeat to fade)

© 1993 Selah Music

****

62

Story Songs

The high school kids in my town used to tailgate on the town square because there was no other place to hang. Although they weren't especially rowdy, the town later imposed a curfew to discourage gatherings there. This song is two stories in one.

Nothing Ever Happens in This Town
Not much ever happens in this town
That's what kids from here say all the time
And tonight's no different—just hanging around
Nothing ever happens in this town

But in a faraway place—a miscalculation
A missile leaves the launching pad
And if allowed to run its course
It'll take out everything in its path

Sitting in the back of Smitty's old truck
There's talk about finals that are coming up
After graduation it all winds down
Cause nothing ever happens in this town

Pilots scramble—take to the air
From an airbase outside Atlanta
The mission's clear—to intercept
Whatever's heading west towards Alabama

Cruisin' the square as the moon comes up
Discussing the usual high school stuff
Who made the team—who's going to prom
And why nothing ever happens in this town

Fighter squadron high above the clouds
Lasers waiting to lock on
Mission control sweats out the clock
A voice comes over the intercom

Light a Creative Fire

Sir, we have it in our sights
Request permission to proceed
We're locked and loaded and at your command
We'll blow this thing to kingdom come

A blinding flash lights up the sky
Thank the good Lord it was eight miles high
Those kids in Alabama went home safe and sound
Yeah, nothing ever happens in this town

We honor those who keep the peace
And hold American soil as our sacred ground
Whoever threatens—we'll hunt them down
And make sure nothing ever happens in this town
Nothing ever happens in this town

© 2005, 2019 Selah Music

****

****

"Being a star means that you just find your own special place and
shine right where you are." —Dolly Parton

****

Whimsy and Frictionless Fiction

I wrote this lullaby after my kids were grown. I can't tell you why...

Sweet Dreams
Let's go to Candyland
Just you and me
Where cotton candy clouds float
Over a root beer sea

We'll live in an Oreo cookie house
There's always something good to eat
When you live on the corner of
Peanut butter and Jelly Street

Sweet dreams in Candyland
Sweet sweet dreams
Sweet dreams in Candyland
Sweet sweet dreams

We'll lick the lollipop trees
Sip from a soda pop fountain
Ride the graham cracker animals
Around marshmallow mountain

Light a Creative Fire

You and me in Candyland
Simply sounds delicious
But you know I'd trade them all
For the sugar in one of your kisses

Sweet dreams in Candyland
Sweet sweet dreams
Sweet dreams in Candyland
Sweet... sweet...
Dreams

****

Morning light (Susie Meyer)

Light a Creative Fire

"A gentleman is someone who knows how to play the banjo and doesn't." —Mark Twain

Joyride
Come along—better buckle up—'cause we're ready to go
Picked this little number up over on Music Row
It's got four-wheel pedal steel and a fiddle with powerglide
Gonna take this beauty for a little spin
C'mon get inside
We're goin' for a joyride
Gonna take a little joyride

It's got a little Merle Haggard in the shape of the lines
You'll hear some Bill Monroe the way the transmission whines
When the twin guitars are kickin' in—this thing's gonna fly
Gonna take this little hummer on down the road
We're goin' for a joyride
Come along for a joyride

(instrumental)

Bridge:
Leave your worries by the side of the road
Let the music take you away
Long as it leaves you satisfied
You know we'll keep on playin'
Cause we love to play
Goin' for a joyride

Better wave – there's ol' George in his Possum mobile
There's Waylon and Willie in a souped-up Coupe de Ville
Along comes Johnny Cash in a long black limousine
With Dolly, Reba and Emmylou like back-seat beauty queens

Whimsy and Frictionless Fiction

Goin' for a joyride
C'mon get inside
We're goin' for a joyride

****

Light a Creative Fire

The genre is rockabilly, a style I grew up with. I was a kid in Michigan listening to Randy's Record Shop on WLAC, a 50,000-watt station from Nashville. Little did I know that I'd one day end up there. Picture Jerry Lee Lewis singing this as he pounds away on his piano...

Burgers and Fries

Every time I see those neon lights blinkin'
That's when my troubles begin
Can't blame a man for what he's thinkin'
Can't pass by without stoppin' in
Some can say no but I'm not that strong
Somethin' that good can't be that wrong
I've got a hankerin' I can't disguise
Gotta have some burgers and fries

Chorus:
Man I love 'em – burgers and fries
It's what I'm thinkin'—when I fantasize
Got my blinker on—gonna drive in
Pay my money down—get my ticket
To hamburger heaven—that ain't no lie
Any way you want 'em
Them burgers and fries

Got my order in—I'm standin' in line
They're flippin' burgers at just the right time
Tuckin' 'em in together – you know side by side
Come and get it – burgers and fries

(Instrumental)

Mondays—I get 'em smothered in onions
Tuesdays—with pickle and grey poupon
Wednesday—two for one with a coupon
Thursdays—I'm home grillin' my own
Fridays—by the bagful—that's no lie
Goin' goin' gone
Burgers and fries
©2001,2019 Selah Music

Whimsy and Frictionless Fiction

Someone once said, "A good teacher is like a candle – it consumes itself to light the way for others." This story tells what happened when someone's life was impacted by the presence of the Great Teacher.

Zacchaeus

A long time ago in Jericho
Zacchaeus was up to no good
He had a large amount in his bank account
He was taxing people more than he should
Now Zacchaeus stood about this tall
People made fun of his size
No one wanted to be his friend
It made him sad inside

One day he heard Jesus was coming
He hurried to the marketplace
He climbed the branches of a sycamore
Just to see Jesus' face
The crowd cried out, "Hey Zacchaeus
Now we can look up to you."
But the laughing stopped and they made a way
So Jesus could come on through and he said

Zacchaeus – come down from the tree
Zacchaeus – you matter to me
I love the rich and poor, young and old
Big and small, the short and the tall
Zacchaeus – invite me in
Zacchaeus – I'll be your friend
Come down from the tree and follow me
Zacchaeus

So Jesus was his guest that day
And when He had gone on his way
Zacchaeus began cleaning up his act
Instead of taking money he was giving it back

Light a Creative Fire

People asked him how can this be
He said Jesus changed my heart and my heart
changed me
Now I give to the poor
Here beneath the sycamore

Zacchaeus – come down from the tree
Zacchaeus – you matter to me
I love the rich and poor, young and old
Big and small, the short and the tall
Zacchaeus – invite me in
Zacchaeus – I'll be your friend
Come down from the tree and follow me
Zacchaeus

****

Whimsy and Frictionless Fiction

"I started in rock music and worked my way up to country."
—Conway Twitty

Trudy Truly
Well I never met a girl quite like Trudy
All my buddies they say the same
She likes riding in my old pickup truck
She don't mind goin' fishin' in the rain

She not much on fancy restaurants
A burger at Sonic suits her fine
She never complains about her clothes
She never ever changes her mind

Chorus:
Trudy—truly
She's my brown-eyed beauty
Just for taking me the way I am
Oh Trudy – her wet kiss is
As good as it gets
She's restored my faith in love again

She never whines about my paycheck
She hates to shop – never talks on the phone
Goin' huntin' is her idea of fun
Trudy you're a rare one

When I'm out with the boys and I leave her alone
She's always happy to see me when I get home
I'd have to say she's my best friend
She's everything you could have been

Chorus:
Trudy – truly
You're amazing to me
Just for letting me be the way I am

Light a Creative Fire

Oh Trudy – you're truly
A man's best friend
With those skinny lips – those floppy ears
And that silly grin

****

Dowsing (Fred Nagelbach)

Light a Creative Fire

Visiting a black church left my wife and me with an unforgettable experience of worship with our brothers and sisters in the faith. A fifty-voice choir, band, tambourines, and a message delivered we still recall, "God Enables Us."

Jump for Joy
It's the day of celebration
The hour is drawing near
It could be any moment
When the guest of honor will appear

So you wait and you wonder
When will the rejoicing start
Never thinking to begin
The celebration in your heart

(Jump for joy) – while you've been waiting
(Jump for joy) – for his song to start
(Jump for joy) – It's already playing
The celebration's in your heart

Careful now – joy is contagious
Those around you will surely know
You might become courageous
You might just want to let it show

Today just like always
His love will lead you on
Because he set your life to music
And Jesus is your sweetest song

(Jump for joy) – go ahead clap your hands
(Jump for joy) – His love will lead you on
(Jump for joy) – He set your life to music
And Jesus is your sweetest song

Rap Break:
You feel the gloom soon as you walk in the room /
Trouble hangin' like a cloud / Head bowed / Big
frown / No hope of reachin' higher ground / Took a
wrong turn on a dark and downward path / Forgot
how to laugh / Life much too serious / So I just give
'em a smile / The hope to cope / Cuz I've been
there too / And friends have pulled me through /
especially my friend Jesus / Cuz when I hear he's
comin' soon / I forget the doom and the gloom /
and think of the place he's makin' for this homeboy
/ It makes me jump for joy...

(Jump for joy) – go ahead clap your hands
(Jump for joy) – His love will lead you on
(Jump for joy) – He set your life to music
And Jesus is your sweetest song

© 2007, Selah Music

****

Romantic themes

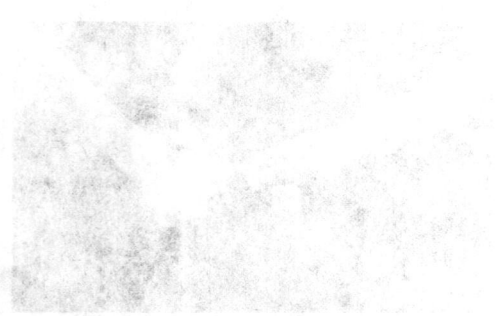

Street Ballads
and
Romantic Themes

"One thing I ask of the Lord, this is what I seek: that I may dwell in the house of the Lord all the days of my life, to gaze upon the beauty of the Lord and seek him in his temple" (Psalm. 27:4).

Flash of Beauty
A song flies away
As soon as it is sung
Caught up by the wind
Never to be heard again
But the words left behind
Take on a life of their own
Like a seed when it's sown
Carries a promise

Chorus:
Will it say to you
Whatever is timeless and true
Will you sing it to your wounded heart
Will it give you just enough
Of what you long to see
A glimpse of hope
A flash of beauty

Dreams never meant to fade

Light a Creative Fire

Are scattered into space
When all they ever needed
Was a soft place to land
Undaunted by the dark
The faintest ray of hope comes
Crashing through the silence
A flash of beauty (Repeat Chorus)

Bridge:
All the words of all the songs
All the hope of what's to come
Is found in you
My flash of beauty
All the moments of all my days
All I give is all my praise
Until you come for me

In a flash of beauty

© 2008, Selah Music

* *

Thinking beach

* *

"Your life as a Christian should make non-believers question their disbelief in God." —Dietrich Bonhoeffer

* *

"That Love is all there is, is all we know of Love..."—Emily Dickinson

Coat of Many Colors
Threads of nations / woven since creation
From tribes and tongues and countries around the world
Placed on their shoulders / a coat of many colors
All blended together / to make a beautiful world

Oh sing your alleluias—in any language
Lift your hosannas—'til they rise above
Show your colors—your coat of many colors
We're all knit together by the bonds of love
Wear it proudly—'cause we all
We all need love

We're woven into / different shapes and sizes
Yet we're so alike in our diversity
But when we blend with others / we make a rainbow of colors
Sending up our hope / for all humanity

Oh sing your alleluias—in any language
Lift your hosannas—'til they rise above
Show your colors—your coat of many colors
We're all knit together by the bonds of love
Wear it proudly—'cause we all
We all need love—(go on)

Blending with others / makes a rainbow of colors
Holding out a hope someday we'll all be free
Blending with others / makes a rainbow of colors
Holding out a hope someday we'll all be free

So Sing.... Sing your alleluias
Your hosannas – 'til they rise above
Wear your colors – your coat of many colors

Light a Creative Fire

Come together – love one another
Like sisters—like brothers
Wear it proudly
'Cause we all need love
© 2017 Selah Music

****

Beneath the deep (Linda Kauth)

Love is fragile. It can blossom when it's well cared for, but sometimes it can fade, for reasons no one can explain. But ask anyone whether love is worth pursuing, and the answer will be… always.

One Inch Deep (and a Mile Wide)

Once we walked in the sunshine
We used to sing in the rain
But lately we've had one-word conversations
And maybe I'm the one to blame

Now whenever we're together
You've got that faraway look in your eyes
I see your lips moving but what you're sayin'
Is one inch deep and a mile wide

The tide is rising – but this ship is sinking
Should I bail or should I let it ride
Oh for a flood of your forgiveness
To fill this emptiness I have inside

As I drown in my self- pity
Hoping love can turn the tide
I nod my head but what you're sayin'
Is one inch deep and a mile wide

Clinging to the final moments
You've already said goodbye
'Cause I find every word you're sayin'
Is one inch deep and a mile wide

© 2019 Selah Music

****

Street Ballads and Romantic Themes

I wrote this from a first-hand experience. Breaking up and making up... All these years later we still tease each other about it.

underdog

Come in out of the cold where we can see you
No need to stand there shivering at the door
Looks like you've been wounded
Did she bruise your ego
She was way out of your league
But you kept coming back for more

Chorus:
That's what it's like when you're the underdog
Licking old wounds that never seem to heal
We won't say we told you so
She put you down she laid you low
Now your back where you belong
underdog

Was it her jasmine perfume or her daddy's money
That made you lose your head and fall in a swoon
On this side of town we know
All about her kind
You're better off being a has-been
Than howling at the moon

She's the one born on the wrong side of the tracks
When you're done mopin' and layin' on the porch
We'll take you back

'Cause that's what it's like when you're the underdog
It won't be long those wounds are gonna heal
You'll be out running with the pack
She'll be begging you to take her back
But you'll be too smart for that
underdog
© 2001 Selah Music

Question: Who was fired from a newspaper for "lacking imagination" and "having no original ideas"?

Answer: Walt Disney

* *

* *

"All the gifts and talents we have are from God, but they are also for God... for his glory and for his pleasure. Don't waste them; make great use of them and make him proud."
—*Amari Cooper, Alabama wide receiver now playing in the NFL*

* *

Street Ballads and Romantic Themes

David wrote many beautiful psalms in the Bible to celebrate his deep relationship with God. If he were to write them today, this is what they might be like.

You Complete Me
You're the rhythm to my dance
You're the blue to my sky
You're the answer to my riddle
You're the apple to my eye
You're the pathway to my journey
You're hands on my every need
When life becomes a puzzle
You complete me

You're the wheel to my turning
First responder to my S O S
You're the rest to my restless heart
The wisdom to my cluelessness
You're the slingshot to my Goliaths
No nothing will ever defeat me
'Cause you complete me

Bridge:
Every time I turn it over
My life is on the mend
I let you hold it for a while
But then I take it back again
Make of me what you will
What you want me to be
Every time I turn it over
You complete me

You're the wind to my sails
The anchor to my storm
You're the moon and stars to the nighttime
The sunrise every morning
You're the who of who I am

Light a Creative Fire

What I was meant to be
Cause you complete me

You're the dance to my feet
You're the blue to my sky

© 2019 Selah Music

****

"If you found out you were dying, would you be nicer, love more, try something new? Well, you are. We all are." —Hippie Peace Freaks

I Come Running

Bare feet splashing / waves along the shore
As the surf glides in / my footprints disappear
Sandpipers scurry / and the seagulls cry
And I come running

Down the distant shoreline / through the morning mist
Someone's coming towards me / I'm not sure who it is
Can it be / my heart is saying it's true
Here I come running
I come running to you

Daring to come closer / realizing you're for real
As I run towards you / the earth is standing still
Will I be welcome / like the prodigal son
I come running
I come running to you

All I ever needed / down to my very breath
Was the life you gave me / saving me from certain death
And just like you promised / you've come to take me home
Here I come running

Down the distant shoreline / out of the morning mist
Someone's coming towards me / and I know who it is
Just like you promised / you've come to take me home
Here I come running
I come running to you

I have a message / for the ones I leave behind
Be ready 'cause he's coming / in these shifting sands of time
Someday we'll be together / and when I see you again
I'll come running

Light a Creative Fire

I'll come running to you

Bare feet splashing
Through the waves along the shore
Surf comes rolling in
And my footprints disappear

© 2009, Selah Music

* *

* *

Joel Rosenberg said, "I don't know what the future holds, but I know who holds the future."

Thank God today for having written your life's story.
You're living it now!

* *

Sipping Stones (Fred Nagelbach)

David's Harp—Blog Favorites

I've never been a fan of the term "blogging." It sounds too much like an unhealthy condition, as in "someone HELP him, he's lying there blogging!" This hasn't deterred me from writing a blog and sending it out every two or three weeks for the last five years. If you insist on following these musings, you can look on my website and subscribe. *(playdavidsharp.com)* And please, don't ask me who David Sharp is.

Whiff

It's a hot, dusty Kansas night... Whiff! The sound of my bat colliding with thin air.

"Striiiike!"

"C'mon son, keep your eye on the ball!" my coach calls out from the first base line.

Feeling the pressure to get a hit after whiffing three straight times the last time up.

"Ball outside," barks the umpire, who carries a whiskbroom to sweep off home plate in one back pocket and a pint in the other.

"Good eye—good eye," encourages our side of the fence. They're counting on me.

The pitcher gives me the evil eye from the mound, shakes off a sign, then nods.

Zing! "Foul ball—strike two!"

"Just a little hit, son. Give it a ride."

I'll be given a ride on the bench if I strike out. I focus on the next ball so hard I see the stitches. I swing for the fences.

Whack! A towering fly ball to left—up, up, up...into a Rawlings fielder's glove.

Inning over.

In my early teens, everything was possible. I was invincible! Goals *galore.* My American dream was a MLB contract to play for the Cardinals. As I matured, that goal faded like a pop fly to left. Everything pointed to my skills being only above average, not major league material. I began to realize *everything* was measured: grade points, wins and losses, votes, business success, popularity poles, IQs.

But there, mixed in with cold reality, was a slow turning towards my modest gifts and skills that showed glimpses of promise. A plan was at work nudging me towards people and events and circumstances that were the right fit. An invisible guiding hand was shaping my life. Finally, I stopped measuring my performances; I asked God to help me focus on Him. Don't ask why it took so long.

Recently, I led the singing and a Bible study in prison ministry. I held up a book for the inmates: "Pretend this book is titled *The Story of Your Life.*" It has a plot, characters, a setting, plenty of drama. Think of each chapter as a year in your life. Some books will have 25 chapters, some 75... or even 85. The question is—what chapter are you in? At what age do you focus on Christ?

Before you were born, He planned the events in your life— your growing up years, your marriage, your life's work, how your life will end. And when. Do you know whose you are?"

"For we are God's masterpiece. He has created us anew in Christ Jesus, so we can do the good things he planned for us long ago" (*Eph. 2:10*). God said that? His masterpiece?

He's the one that pleads for you, "C'mon son, keep your eye on the ball." How awesome the world becomes when you carry out His plans in the light of the cross.

You'll still whiff the ball, or foul it back, or strike out. That's life. Get in the game!! Step up to the plate with confidence and face the exciting challenges He places in your path.

Whack! "It's a well-hit ball, going deep...back...back...back..."

****

The Irrepressible Cross

We searched every crevice and unzipped every compartment of our luggage. Retraced every step up to the last time I wore it. Nothing of great value really, just a small cross made of three nails on a silver-linked chain.

I left a message at the desk to see if housekeeping would check behind the dresser, the last place I recall seeing it, but it never turned up. Because of its personal value, a gift from my wife years ago, I'm not sure I can replace it. Or want to...

When I was in my teens, I must confess to feeling weird when our family went somewhere in public, and my father, a local pastor, wore his clerical collar. It's the same uneasiness I feel now whenever people with tattoos wear sleeveless tank tops to show their ink. Or when a rock star wears a crucifix the size of a cereal box.

Is the purpose of wearing a cross to identify with others of the faith, or is it to make a statement? Is it a trendy fashion piece? Perhaps a way to ward off evil spirits? W.W.J.D?

It's interesting that Jesus during his ministry told the disciples numerous times not to mention the miracles he did to anyone. I believe it was his divine, understated way to tell his followers He wanted to be known as more than a healer, more than a teacher; he wanted people to come to him, not simply for the benefits, but to come for a relationship... with himself and with his Father.

I've never had a problem with athletes who make the sign of the cross before they go to bat, or before they receive a kickoff, or have a holy huddle after a game with their teammates. That, to me, is worship; that's prayer. So if someone has a fish symbol on their hatchback, or praying hands bookends on their shelf, who am I to judge what may help them focus on their personal faith?

Years ago, during a Lenten service, we were given a small piece of paper and a nail when we entered the sanctuary. We were asked to write the things we were struggling with on the piece of paper and, one by one, pick up a hammer and nail it to a wooden cross. It was to remind us: It was our sins that put Christ there, and they were paid for.

Every Easter Sunday, we're asked to bring flowers to adorn a cross we put up along the roadside in front of our church. What a tacit, glorious statement! Gray dead wood is transformed into a display of vivid spring flowers. From ashes we find beauty; from death we find life.

The now-empty cross and its timeless story keeps turning up in our daily lives, through the Word and by God's design, always in the hope that the world will come to know of its tragic beauty and embrace it. The Spirit of God runs deep, seeping over the walls we build that cannot contain it, permeating life of those who claim him or don't, offering Jesus and his resurrection life to all.

I hope someone does find the cross I lost and is wearing it with dignity and humbleness, and that it helps remind them what the cross stands for.

Maybe the plan all along was that I lose that cross so a certain someone would find it. I'll never know, but I know one thing: God works in mysterious ways. He took a symbol of Roman execution, and transformed it into the ultimate icon of eternal life.

****

Inspiration

For the Love of Pete

Pete was a rare bird. In a good way, I mean. He talked with a faint whistle-y voice; you had to lean in so you could hear him when he spoke. And Pete always had something to say in his raspy voice – some of it nonsense, for he was full of fantasies and some not quite fully-baked ideas.

Many times you were deliberating when you saw him, whether to let him approach you or turn away, for he came bearing his secrets, or his latest poem – or his wisdom. For Pete was no fool. He married an Italian woman twice his size who had her own agenda, and she could spar with the best of them, especially when Pete was in the ring.

Pete always carried around a handkerchief to wipe his dewy eyes. At least I thought that was the reason, until I came to realize it was a perpetual gleam, because Pete was always working on something, and he could hardly wait to let you in on it.

He wrote letters to presidents. He composed letters to movie stars, to country music artists, and head of corporations he had read about in the papers. For Pete had a gift. He was hardly able to get a word in edgewise due to the verbosity of his significant other who often spoke *for* him rather than *to* him. So his gift, to anyone who would listen, became his

101

poetry. Pete loved to share. It was his nature to divulge his thoughts, some of which were maybe left too long on the stove.

Pete was the arch-typical Italian who loved to share what he had cooked up. Food for thought...Food for the soul...Comfort food. He had this great appetite to express himself; it was his genetic compulsion to share with others whether they agreed with him or not. Because that was the whole beauty of putting it on paper: he had his say and no one could tell him otherwise. His personal view of the world was his own and, having expressed it, nothing was up for discussion, nor could it be refuted.

There were other ways Pete gave of himself to others. It was in rather strange ways to some, but so totally appropriate once you knew what Pete was about. He was a solid citizen, and therefore he decided to offer his services to his community—for free. He made it his business to pick up other people's trash along the road, and when he had a bagful, took it to the dumpster at McDonald's. A good deal of it probably came from there anyway. He may have made a few bucks from the cans he collected, but that wasn't the reason he did it. Pete saw a need in his neighborhood and he set about getting it accomplished.

Hard to tell whether picking up after people affected his health or his posture, for in his later years he became stooped over and walked that way, and when you saw him you wanted to rush over and make sure he would get where he was going, all the while hoping a strong wind wouldn't blow him over.

Pete is no longer with us; he passed on a number of years ago. I think he would have been proud to know one more letter was written about the world according to Pete, one that can now be added to the many he wrote. He's probably sitting on a park bench in heaven right now writing his next poem. He is standing up nice and straight, and yes he still has a twinkle in his eye, even more so.

All the people – the ones that made it to heaven – presidents, movie stars and corporate chiefs that Pete wrote letters to on earth are now coming up to him so they could shake his hand. "So you're the one who wrote me that letter! I recall you were also a poet..." And since it *is* heaven, Pete now has equal say and is living in perfect harmony with Ma, the love of his earthly life.

The two of them—Pete and Rose were beautiful in their own way, a way that will never be duplicated. They were as different as night and day.

And as unique as God ever made two people.

Who's Packing Your Parachute?

t was a call from my wife, and it sounded urgent. "We have to leave as soon as you get home; we're off to get your birthday present." I had no clue what that meant; my big 5-0 was several days away. I picked her up and we drove to the high school field where a multi-colored hot air balloon was in the process of being inflated. We were the passengers! We met our pilot David, who called us two days early to take advantage of the day's calm winds and bright sun.

A distinct smell of propane was in the air as the burners slowly righted the balloon until the gondola, which was tied down, rested underneath it. We piled in with David, the taunt ropes were undone, and we lifted off into the great beyond. No oxygen, no seat belt, no parachute, only a champagne split and two glasses.

David threw tiny lead balls with pink streamers over the side to see where the wind currents would take us. We were in luck, for the prevailing winds headed us north towards our neighborhood. We topped out at eleven hundred feet, and it was, in a word, breathtaking. With the late-April trees carpeting the hills, the rolling green earth below reminded me of ...(*I know this sounds dumb*) a head of broccoli.

My wife and I had never met David before that day, or since. His card certified him as a professional balloonist, one that would get us up safely, but just as importantly, bring us safely back down to terra firma.

I was half joking with him about the parachutes, realizing after the fact that a chute from the heights we were sailing would never open in time. That's gravity for ya.

This experience begs the question: should we have done a background check? What if David, our pilot, only got two out of five stars? When you board a plane, you don't shake hands with the pilot. When you get on the interstate, you have to believe those you share the road with are trustworthy. You check your tires and buckle up your seatbelt to increase your odds, but just about all of life is putting your trust in something, or someone.

Doing life requires many leaps of faith: a marriage, a job, having surgery, raising a family, national security, the bridge you cross every day on the way home. When you realize how little control you have over your circumstances, that you're living in an unstable world, take great comfort in knowing the one who knew you before the world began, the one whose offer still stands: *Come to me... and I'll give you rest.*

The truth of the matter finally becomes real when we come to the end of ourselves and release all the junk we've been carrying around that makes us sick with worry and stress. Our faithful God and his Son Jesus took your burdens and mine to the cross. Maybe it's time we left them there.

How many times has God spared your life? Three thousand years ago, King David offered a promise for our life and times: *"Give your burdens to the Lord, and he will take care of you. He will not permit the godly to slip and fall."* (Psalm 55:22 *NLT*)

When God asks you to take a leap of faith, and you weigh your options whether to handle it yourself or turn it over, remember his faithful promises to you in His Word. As for the baggage of this world you're trying to carry—let it go. God has packed your parachute with such great mercy and hope, and in such abundance, you will land exactly where He wants you to be. *Lo, I am with you always...*

Turn your leaps of faith over to the One who's packing your parachute. And welcome... to the great wide open!

****

In his image (Fred Nagelbach)

What Happens in Vegas...

S omewhere in the world of advertising is a copywriter who was promoted to his agency's corner office for coming up with a campaign for Las Vegas tourism that says, "What happens in Vegas – stays in Vegas." Nothing could be further from the truth. The one time I made the trip for a convention was fun, but personally, I felt uneasy. "C'mon, don't be a prude... it's just about folks having a good time." Yet, I would be naive if I didn't recognize the undercurrent of darkness that lurks there, a minefield of stuff not good for me. Feeling invincible?

David was king of Israel, and things were going swimmingly. He led so many successful tours of duty against hostile nations, he deservingly took some R&R.

One sultry night, David couldn't sleep because of the heat. Hoping he would find a breeze, he stepped out on the veranda, and looking down over the city, he got an eyeful – Bathsheba was bathing on the rooftop below. You know the rest of the story. What happens in Jerusalem – stays in Jerusalem. Right? Picture the Deceiver in the shadows calmly filing his talons.

Along with adultery, the convenient death of Uriah, Bathsheba's husband, comes David's denial of wrongdoing. He was the unimpeachable king who was above the law and therefore had no need to repent. After all, he was endorsed and anointed by God, even called *"the man after God's own heart."*

Then the luxury of misery began. Denial and self-pity started their pursuit. Marinating in self-loathing, he sulked around the palace; some scholars say it was as long as a year. He couldn't face his kingly duties, couldn't worship or write or sing praises to a God he refused to face.

> *My heart pounds, my strength fails me*
> *The light has gone from my eyes*
> *I've become my own worst enemy*
> *Pierced with arrows You let fly*
> *("Pronto Viene Jesu Cristo" from David's Harp CD)*

This chapter in David's life is God's wakeup call—not only to tell David's story, warts and all, but to warn about a rebellious nature lurking *in us.* When unforgiveness or guilt get us down in the dumps, what Oswald Chambers calls the luxury of misery, our moods are only overcome by kicking them out. When the Deceiver hears the prayer, *"In the name of Christ— get out of my face!",* he *must* leave your spirit.

With forgiveness comes transformation. And oh, what a sweet relief when you and I and David place our feet on the road to recovery!

"Finally, I confessed all my sins to you and stopped trying to hide my guilt. I said to myself, 'I will confess my rebellion to the Lord.' And you forgave me! All my guilt is gone" (Ps. 32:5-6 *NLT*).

Misery loves company, and there are naysayers all around that would like to drown you in their misery. *Don't let them!* Try to bring them to that place of restoration you too once needed, and tell them that, although you feel their pain, there is a holy remedy. Show them hope in a God that receives his prodigal sons and daughters with His mighty open arms.

David says in Psalm 51:2: *"Restore to me the joy of your salvation, and uphold me by your generous Spirit."* (*NKJV*) Someone who knows about fighting depression and misery said, "Don't tell God how big your storm is; tell the storm how big your God is."

****

A waiting table

The Spider and the Fly

I t hung suspended above a grassy slope, catching the sunlight filtering through the trees. A perfect web the size of a basketball with no apparent tether other than a tree branch ten feet above. How brilliant the construction, how perfectly suited to trap its prey and provide a juicy morsel for a spider's dinner.

With the same predator instinct, you and I often become the unsuspecting prey of those whose intentions are to entice you, to entrap you. Who are the conspirators of such entanglements? Hucksters, smooth operators, solicitors who want to convince you that you need what they're selling: the best investment, the lowest price, the secret formula to grow hair, the diet that really, really works!

I'm not throwing shade on our human existence as if it were flimsy fiction. You'll recall what the first letters of any website stand for: w.w.w. = World Wide Web. The information highway. (*Thank you Al Gore*) We've become cannon fodder for the spammers. I have no ax to grind, as some do; those who call the Internet the devil's plaything, which it can be. But consider this...

In a recent interview with the critical minds of Silicon Valley who were instrumental in creating the first prototypes of the internet, cellphones, and software models of commonly used programs today, the developers admitted one result that left them aghast: what a habit-forming monster their inventions have become. They opened a Pandora's box that has spawned a new world order; one that's being upgraded at warp speed. There is no turning back. It can make those of us who lived B.D. (*before digital*) feel very small, entangled in a web of relentless "progress."

In spite of what all the world offers, something is amiss. In the name of self-sufficiency, God's role has been back-burnered, and don't think He's okay with that.

Welcome to life in the cosmos that neither asks for, nor gives consideration to spiritual wisdom in the choices people make, or the way they do life.

You can't blame the spider for instinctively building a web so he can survive. Neither can you deny humanity the search for a true identity in the One who created them. The need for God was written on your heart and mine, in every human being. Scripture condemns those who enslave, ensnare, and prey on people who are vulnerable, weak, or in need. Sin alienates, separates us from Him.

Because of this worldwide abuse, we have our marching orders. It's time to assemble under His banner of love. We are to be salt and light in a tasteless, darkening world. We're to be as wise as serpents and as gentle as doves.

Defender of the faith is our job description, for there's a Ruler we are required to measure all things by. His way is a way of freedom *from* all things that would enslave people with the trappings of darkness. God never intended anyone to exist without a lasting relationship with himself, but it came with a price.

It was paid with the sacrifice of Christ's body and blood. And yes, he took your place and mine when we should have paid the penalty. So now we pay it forward. We seek those who need to be rescued that are caught in the web of the world's fake news.

Freedom from traps and snares in your daily walk with God comes when you're in sync with Him, always ready to receive and dispense the gifts of the Holy Spirit: love, joy, peace, and hope.

David, as paraphrased in Psalm 4 tells us: *"Why is everyone hungry for more? "More, more," they say. "More, more." I have God's more-than-enough, more joy in one ordinary day than they get in all their shopping sprees. At day's end I'm ready for sound sleep, for you, God, have put my life back together. (The Message)*

God is truly enough. Don't live like a victim. Live like a victor, because you are His!

****

Balaam's Talking Donkey

Once upon a time there was a man called Balaam who was hired to pronounce curses on the people of Israel. Balak, the Moabite king, was afraid of being overrun by the Israelites, and he was hoping Balaam's curses would stop them in their tracks.

In spite of a warning from God, Balaam saddled up his donkey to pronounce the curses. Balaam's donkey stopped when he saw an angel of the Lord standing in the road with a drawn sword, and bolted into a field. Balaam, who never saw the angel, had to beat the donkey until he got back on the road.

Two more times the donkey saw the angel vision, and two more times he got beaten, until the donkey, fed up with the beatings, spoke to Balaam saying, "What have I done to you that deserves your beating me three times?'

"You have made me look like a fool!" Balaam shouted. "If I had a sword with me, I would kill you!" (I'm not making this up; it's in the Old Testament – Numbers 22.)

"But I am the same donkey you have ridden all your life," the donkey answered. "Have I ever done anything like this before?"

That's when the Lord opened Balaam's eyes to see the angel of the Lord standing in the road with a drawn sword. Balaam bowed his head and fell face down on the ground before him. He finally got the message God was sending via the donkey.

What's it going to take for God to get *your* attention?

I had a music group years back that I was trying to get record labels to sign as new artists, but no one would give them a listen. Frustrated that no one returned my calls, I mailed a club-sized wooden two by four along with a note saying, "I *hope I don't have to use this on you to get your attention. Here's my number...*" I got a call from the head guy the next day to say they passed, but "we're gonna use your promotion idea; we loved the 2 x4!"

What's it going to take for God to get your attention? A talking donkey? An angel with a flaming sword in the road? A 2 x 4? The answer is... all that heaven will allow, for as you might know, God has no limits. He's full of surprises.

Consider the many ways He reaches out to us to encourage our relationship with him. He calls us his bride. He makes us his children. He describes us as a holy nation, his royal priesthood. He promises an everlasting love. I see my reaction and wonder why I, or anyone else who calls themselves Christian, would be willing to settle for such a small portion of the feast.

I'm convicted by the blandness of my response, my lip service, my going-through-the-motions while at the same time hoping my heart will catch up to the outrageous love he offers. It's my attention span that I question. The spirit is willing, but...

C. S. Lewis noted in *The Weight of Glory:* "It would seem that Our Lord finds our desires not too strong, but too weak. We are half-hearted creatures, fooling about with drink and sex and ambition when infinite joy is offered us, like an ignorant child who wants to go on making mud pies in a slum because he cannot imagine what is meant by the offer of a holiday at the sea. We are far too easily pleased."

Balaam did finally get it right.... much to his donkey's relief. Balaam told King Balak, "I have no power to say whatever I want. I will speak only the message that God puts in my mouth." Balak's response: "Curses, foiled again."

As long as we're walking this earth, we're going to be coerced by the Enemy to cave in to the distractions this world has to offer. I see in this choice of words by C. S. Lewis the wisdom of titling his observations the *Weight* of Glory. Consider the depths, the everlasting riches of on-going grace that is the glory of an awesome God!

The heartfelt promises God lavishes on us should get our attention, the ways he dotes on us and gives us his ever-presence.

It's so obvious, even a donkey can see them.

* *

If you enjoyed reading this book, I'd welcome your comments on the book online at **amazon.com***. Pass this book on to anyone who might benefit from its contents. Now go out and create!*

Accolades

My hope is that this book encourages those who live by their wits, or would like to; who merge their real-life thoughts with fantasy, and think in tangents. Without them, the world would be a duller place. The world needs left-brained people too, for their talents and natural abilities are gifts as well, bringing balance to creative pursuits by providing structure, organization, and appreciation for all things creative. We're all a part of a bigger picture!

Gratitude is the first word that comes to mind for all the people who contributed their talents and skills putting this book together. Calling on long-time friend Joe Ashley to be my editor and make my words behave was a natural choice, and a beneficial one. Placing the formatting in the skillful hands of Loral Pepoon of Selah Press, along with her husband Seth highlighting the photographs made the pages come to life. My discussions with Carl Schoenbeck and Fred Nagelbach were most valuable in solidifying the direction and focus of this book.

Speaking of focus, a big thank you to those who shared their artistic talents and skills shown in the photos that grace these pages: Robin O'Rourke Petersen for her cover photos, Fred Nagelbach for his whimsical creations, Linda Kauth, Barb Schoenbeck, and Susie Meyer for their artistic gifts. A thank you also to those who reviewed this book. The check's in the mail.

Acknowledging last and foremost: that all glory be given to God, the Father of all creation, the Lord Jesus, and the Holy Spirit for their "breathing into" our thoughts and ideas for all things practical, spiritual, artistic, musical, or whimsical.

Notes*

1. Leland Ryken, *The Liberated Imagination: Thinking Christianly About the Arts*, Wheaton Literary Series (Wheaton, Ill.: H Shaw Publishers, 1989).

All other quoted material is believed to be in the public domain.